GREEN ENERGY

GREEN ENERGY

Table of Contents

Chapter 1

Introduction

We have come along way in developing societies that have electricity and the power necessary to fuel vehicles and for industry to be successful. All of these efforts though rely upon the use of energy source that comes from fossil fuels.

They are found in the ground and have to be processed in order for us to have that fuel and that electricity. They are known as coal, natural gas, and fuel. We rely on them way too much for our own good and that is why change is so important.

The problem though is that our dependence on it continues to grow. As more people are upon the Earth than ever before we are using more every single day. People are living longer too due to advances in health care. We are certainly a society dependent upon our electronic gadgets as well.

While those are all good things for us to be happy about, the fact that we are depleting the fossil fuel available isn't. This type of energy source isn't one that we will be able to replace. When it is gone it is gone and that is the reality of the situation.

It won't all disappear during our lifetimes, but it is going to pose a problem for future generations. While efforts can be made to converse fossil fuels, eliminating enough of the use in order to really make a difference isn't going to occur unless we take a close look at some alternative methods.

Society isn't going to go back to using horses and carriages for transportation. They also aren't going to go back to lighting their homes with candles at night. With the computer use around us in homes and for business it isn't even practical to suggest we stop using the electricity that is necessary to allow them to operate.

We can often take for granted just turning the key and our car starts, turning on the thermostat to have heating or cooling in our home, and flipping a switch to give us the lighting we need in any room. Some people are also selfish as they don't care what is going to happen for future generations as long as they have what they need right now.

Luckily, the majority of the population doesn't think that way. They aren't out to use everything they can without looking back. The problem though is that they often don't realize what they are using could be a problem down the road. Even if they do, they may not realize that they have some other options they can try to implement.

Learning about the various types of renewable energy is a great way to get a person thinking about changes they can implement. There have been some significant efforts made in this area but there is still much more than needs to be taking place. Instead of being afraid of what is unknown to you, do your best to learn the basics of all the renewable energy sources possible.

The government of the United States has gotten involved in promoting renewable energy sources as well. They offer some great financial incentives for homes and businesses to you them. Even so, there is sometimes a high overhead to get everything in place. This can prevent many people from being a part of saving our natural resources even when they really would like to.

It is estimated that about 13% of our current energy is the result of renewable energy. With the money to cover the expenses, advanced technology, and a desire by society to continue using them we can see that percentage significantly increase. There are plenty of benefits to renewable energy too such as not harming the environment with pollutants.

If you are asking yourself why we don't just turn to them now the answer isn't that simple. In a nutshell there is still a great deal of research that needs to be completed. There is also the high cost to contend with as well as various disadvantages with each of the types of renewable energy.

If you keep on reading though you will get to this information as well. Then it will make sense as far and the big picture of what we currently get from renewable energy, what the limitations are, and what we can expect into the future. This will help you to understand the benefits as well as the drawbacks of the situation more clearly.

Chapter 2

What is Renewable Energy?

Fossil fuels are used to make energy we use, but once they are gone we will never get more of them. Coal, oil, and natural gas all fall into this category. They are used all over the place in high amounts so you may not realize that they are in limited supply.

These forms of energy have been used mainly because they are affordable and they don't take up very much room to incorporate. They can be transported anywhere they are needed as well. With natural resources there have to be certain elements in place in order to take advantage of them.

The concept of renewable energy embraces the ability to use the resources we naturally have, but that we will never run out of. This way we can continue to have all the benefits we want without destroying the Earth.

We also won't be preventing future generations from having the chance to future grow and evolve beyond what we were able to see take place in our own lifetime. This process involves taking these types of natural resources and turning them into a product we can use for power.

That means a great deal of information and technology has to be collected and evaluated. Many of these methods though continue to see advances in the designs and processing which will result in them being even more valuable in the future than they are right now.

Most will agree that renewable energy sources are better for the environment. The burning of fossil fuels including gasoline and coal isn't good for the environment. These natural resources will allow us to save resources and at the same time to live in a cleaner environment than we have now.

Many believe it isn't practical or safe to depend only upon these types of resources though. That is because the sun doesn't always shine so the energy can't be collected. There are many places where the sun is blocked for days due to the changes in the seasons.

You can't predict how much wind will be produced or how much power can be taken from the water. It will vary significantly but there is no reason why we can't rely upon these renewable energy sources as the primary providers. We can then depend on fossil fuels as back up so we never have to go without the energy we want to use.

Chances are you have heard about the various forms of renewable energy but not in detail. Keep on reading and you will get all the information you need including the pros and cons of each type. You will find each of them does offer some hope for the future though as far as reducing our dependency on those resources which we can't replenish.

Chapter 3

Types of Renewable Energy

When you think about the natural things around us a couple of things come to mind. First, you have the sun that continues to shine brightly in the sky day after day. It gives off a great deal of heat which can be converted into energy. The sun shines brightly some days and then is covered with clouds other days. So the amount of energy you can collect each day is going to vary.

Next, you have water which covers the majority of the surface of the Earth. There is also the additional moisture and rainfall that can be collected as time goes by. There is energy found in the water as it moves along and this can be converted into energy at hydropower plants.

Even if it is just barely there on certain days, you also have the wind. In some areas it is extremely windy all the time. In order for the equipment used to create wind power to be worth the cost it must be blowing most days at a speed of at least 15 miles per hour.

Most people view that as a nuisance but they don't realize the full potential of it. They aren't really aware that the wind that is all around you can be used to create renewable energy. It is also very clean for the environment so you don't have to worry about negative effects from it.

Biofuel is also a source of renewable energy and the one most people know the least about. This concept involves using types of materials that you can burn to create energy. This can be left over paper and wood, trash, and even manure from animals.

It is quite an interesting concept and one you will want to be sure you read about. You can be sure this is one area of renewable energy that will continue to grow by leaps and bounds in the next decade. Don't underestimate how valuable it can be as it also removes waste from our environment. This type of renewable energy is scientific in nature and one that has been around the least amount of time.

Chapter 4

Solar Power

Solar power is likely to be the most valuable of the renewable energy sources available. That is because it is plentiful and it is the least expensive to implement. New buildings can be built that incorporate the concepts as can homes. There are also solar panels that can be added to what is already in place.

That way you can take any home or business and modify it to use solar power with. They can be expensive but you will find that they can be a very good investment. If you own an apartment building with the electricity included in the rent this can help to reduce your overhead expenses. In a couple of years the process will pay for itself.

This process involves placing collectors and panels that will be in places where the sun will reach such as the roof. The process of converting what is collected into energy is known as photovoltaics. In order to make this happen, silicon is used to transform it.

The concept of solar power has also found its way to vehicles. They have cells that capture energy from the sun to provide movement for the vehicle. The advanced design allows that energy to be continually conserved too such as when you come to a stoplight.

If you drive your vehicle for longer than you have enough solar power for you aren't going to be stranded in the middle of the interstate. You also won't find your vehicle shutting off the moment the sun goes down. This is because it also operates on regular gasoline.

The solar energy is always consumed first though before any of the gas is used. You will continue to use the gas for movement until you have replenished the solar energy. Even when you are using the gas though this type of vehicle is going to burn cleaner and thus not place all of the pollutants into the atmosphere that other vehicles do.

Hybrid vehicles are available in quite a few models and more of them seem to be introduced all the time. However, it can be very expensive to be able to purchase one. They cost quite a bit more than other types of vehicles on the market. Yet if you are looking for a great way to rely upon renewable energy sources this is one way to do it.

If you are paying a fortune right now for fuel to keep your current vehicle going it may be most cost effective for you. Even with a higher monthly payment until you pay off the hybrid vehicle you can take the money you save on gas and allocate it towards that payment.

Solar power plants have started to crop up in locations where people never expected them. Both California and Florida have plans to create at least eight new locations each in the next five years in order to generate more of their power from the sunlight.

In fact, California is a leader in promoting the use of solar power. There is a plan in the works to create 3,000 megawatts of it by 2017. The goal of this is to create a way for California to get all the energy they need without using up their natural resources.

Many of the citizens of California aren't happy with the initiative though due to the cost of it. This is a project that will cost almost $3 million before it is completed. Yet the leaders of California are confident it is a step in the right direction. They are confident it will help all of their residents now as well as future generations.

Many people in California though are taking the initiative and running with it. They are being offered very high rates of money back for installing solar panels on their homes and businesses. Construction companies are offered incentives to build new structures with them already in place.

California isn't the only state that is moving forward with incentives for residents though. Check to see if your state is willing to reimburse you for a portion of the cost of having the solar panels installed. This can be a great way for you to save money on the project. At the same time you will be doing your part to cut back on the amount of non-renewable energy your household consumes.

It is vital that we learn do to all we can with collecting solar power. Experts believe that there is more energy from the sun every single day that we can use than what we burn up in fossil fuels annually. That is an amazing evaluation and one that does mean a great deal for the future of all of us.

Just imagine if we were collecting and using a fraction of that amount what we would be able to preserve in regards to our non-renewable resources. You may be asking just what is holding everyone back and the answer is simply the cost that is involved.

Yet as you will notice more and more of it will be taking place and every little bit will be one step closer to really getting the results we are striving for as a society. It is going to take decades for us to get there but that is still better than the alternative. There is no reason to continue depending only on non-renewable energy when we don't' have to.

It is estimated that 20,000 homeowner's in the United States currently get at least 80% of their electricity from solar energy. This saves approximately 50,000 tons of coal each year in order to produce that same amount of power. That is quite a bit of our natural resources being saved from such a small number of people being involved.

Chapter 5

Wind Power

Across the plains where there is open land, the wind is able to move at high speeds. This is due to there not being any buildings or homes in the area to break it up. This is the perfect location for wind power to be generated and collected.

The use of windmills to create energy has been around for a very long time. Of course these windmills were quite small compared to what is out there just to create the energy. Not all spaces are right for large windmills so they look for those where the wind constantly blows at a rate of at least 15 miles per hour.

There are large windmills hundreds of feet high strategically gathered in these open areas. Each of the blades on the windmills requires a semi truck to haul it. They are then put into place with various pieces of construction equipment. They operate on their own but are closely monitored to ensure everything is working like it should on them.

Even though it is a great deal of cost and work to get them installed, each one can last about 20-25 years. That means they are well worth the investment because they don't constantly have to be replaced. That really has been an encouragement for more of them to be put into use.

The collection of wind power has proven to be so profitable in many small towns that some farmers and ranchers have given up those operations. Instead they are allowing various companies to place these windmills on their land and getting paid to do so. They don't have to do any of the work to maintain them and they are guaranteed to make money.

With the high risk involved in the line of farming and ranching, it is understandable why so many of them do it. For those close to retirement age as well it just makes sense to be able to rely on a given income source. This is less stressful than hoping for a good crop in the field or that the price of meat doesn't decline on the market.

Installing these types of windmills to generate the power though is extremely expensive. It is also a time consuming process due to the sheer size of them. When you see them from an airplane or driving down a main highway you won't realize just how enormous they are. On average they are approximately 200 to 250 feet from the ground.

The largest wind turbine in the world is located in Hawaii. It is more than 20 stories high. Each of the blades on the windmills are the size of a full football field. Each of the turbines located here is able to produce enough energy to offer electricity for 300 homes in the area.

If you get a chance though go drive into an area that features them so you can see with your own eyes how they really appear. In Iowa there are approximately 800 of them on what is know as wind farms. More than 200,000 homes are supplied with power from them. You will also find them in Minnesota, Wisconsin, Oklahoma, Kansas, California, and Colorado.

When you watch the turbines spinning you will notice the turn counterclockwise. As the wind blows the shaft is engaged which is connected to a generator. As the blades turn this generator will move the power created along to the locations on the grid. They are monitored and there is an emergency shut off for them as well.

In the event of pending natural disasters such as a tornado, these turbines can give them more power to move on and to destroy everything in its path. By shutting them off that isn't going to be the case.

It can also prevent the blades from being damaged during such an event. With the cost of the windmills being so high, keeping them in good working condition is very important. In some areas tornadoes are a common problem so the windmills are constantly watched.

Not everyone is a fan of these windmills though because they think they are an eyesore. They want to be able to gaze out their window and see the open land. Instead they are seeing tons of windmills. They also feel it takes away the romantic and tranquil feeling of the area.

Yet when you have small towns that are struggling for their residents to make a living, the prospect of getting paid to let a company come in and place windmills in place to collect the energy is an answer to a pray. They would rather have money for food on the table than to have the wide open spaces.

The amount of energy that can be produced this way will never be the same. It can be severely windy one day and only a gentle breeze the next. Even so, there is enough of it to make it worth the cost of getting all the equipment in place. It is worth it to be sharing the natural beauty of an area as well.

Some of these turbines are also located in various bodies of water. It is believed that wind power could one day be responsible for about 50% of the energy we consume. There is still a great deal of research and development that must take place for it to happen.

Yet it is very exciting to know such a renewable energy resource can be there for us. It can make us breath easier when we continue how much of our natural resources that we can't replace continue to be consumed each and every day.

The fact that it doesn't release anything negative into the environment is very important as well. The fact that here isn't carbon dioxide and other gases going into the air as wind power is produced should mean a great deal to each of us. It means the air we breathe is healthier for us than it was before.

The American Wind Energy Association has continued to work to get this type of renewable energy in place around the country. Many find it strange that other countries including Spain and Germany rely on it more than the United States does. However, with the positive aspects of it you can expect the volume of it used here to continue increasing annually.

According to their estimates, we can create 1 ½ times the amount of electricity used annually in the United States based on the amount of wind that is out there daily on average. That is very exciting news and something that could really help us to preserve our natural resources to the best of our ability.

There have been some animal rights groups pointing out that the spinning turbines on these windmills is seriously injuring and even killing various types of birds. To evaluate these claims there have been some studies in place.

Efforts are being made to prevent this without reducing the effectiveness of the wind energy that is being produced. It is believed that these incidents are very limited though and that birds aren't in any real danger due to the turbines out there creating energy.

Chapter 6

Hydropower

There is also power found in water and that process is referred to as hydropower. It can create much more energy at one time than either solar power or wind power. This is due to the fact that water is so dense.

Therefore it only takes a little bit of water to create some power. It takes much more sunlight or wind to create that same amount. Hydropower is used to offer electricity to more than 28 million people around the world. It accounts for approximately 10% of all the electricity produced in the United States.

The process involves plenty of safety precautions as the water can never come into contact with the electrical part of the process. We all know that can spell disaster. The process occurs as the water flows and it spins turbines that are found in a generator.

While this process isn't new, it has been upgraded since it was first used thousands of years ago. The Egyptians were a very smart society and they were able to use it to grind down their grains. It was also used as a way to saw wood as it kept the blades cool enough.

The first hydro power plant in the United States was introduced in 1882. It was placed in Wisconsin. Most people don't realize that a great deal of the early electricity and power in the United States once came from such hydropower plants. In 1940 approximately half of the electricity used came from this source. Later it was replaced by the use of coal.

Of course that was before we knew that coal was something that we will one day run out of. We didn't realize at that time just how much of it we were going to be using. We also didn't realize how much it was going to pollute our environment. It seems ironic that to move forward we have to go back but that is how it plays out in this particular case.

There are several dams in the United States where elaborate designs are in place. Here huge volumes of power are generated each day using these methods. It is a very time consuming and complex process though to turn water into energy. Since hydropower is so expensive it isn't as widely used as it could be.

The largest hydropower plant in the world is located in Washington along the Grand Coulee Dam. It took 11 years to build it from 1933 to 1942. Since that time it has undergone numerous facelifts and changes. It is amazing at a size of over 5,000 feet long and 550 feet high.

In all there are four distinct power plants found here. Each one is controlled separately for easier control of the process to make energy. There are 33 generators and more that 2 million homes in that area get their energy from this particular location. It is an amazing accomplishment and one that really shows the power that can be created with such a renewable energy source.

Some of the newer approaches for hydropower include generating that power from the waves in the ocean. Even the waves that occur all day long in the waters there can be used to create energy. It is believed that the use of hydropower will one day be much more significant than it is right now.

Of course it doesn't make sense for hydropower to be used everywhere. There are many places where there just isn't enough water flowing in the area for them to work well. Not every place as an abundance of rivers, streams, and oceans to produce hydropower. Most of them are found along the West of the United States. They are in Oregon, Washington, and California.

If a way to convert that energy from the water can be found that is less expensive than what we know right now it surely will. It only makes sense due to the volumes of energy that can be created from this particular natural resource. It also doesn't reduce the amount of water out there or place any type of harmful contaminants into it.

There is research though that indicates the aquatic live forms in the waters may be affected by the process. It can upset the natural balance of what ordinarily goes on in that water. There is also the risk of terrorism in an event to destroy what we have built.

Since the events of 09/11 tighter security efforts have been implemented in order to prevent that from happening. There are random checkpoints and stops along the way where vehicles are inspected. There are also restrictions at places including Hoover Dam that prevent large trucks and buses from going across them as an additional safety precaution.

It can take years to build the dams for a hydroelectric plant to start operating though. Many people who live in the vicinity of a proposed hydroelectric plant aren't happy about it either. They worry about flooding and they often find their homeowner's insurance goes up due to that possibility.

Chapter 7

Biofuel

Biofuel isn't one of the well known types of renewable energy but an important one to understand. The process begins when plants to through photosynthesis. There is chemical energy stored inside of it that can be released. What they create is a type of biomass and that can be turned into fuel.

It can then be burned in combustible engines. There is still plenty of research that needs to be done in the area of biofuel. The process right now of converting it isn't as effective as it should be. It is also extremely time consuming and expensive to do so.

Biofuel can be in the form of a liquid or a solid. Vegetable oil that is used as an alternative fuel source for some vehicles out there is a type of liquid biofuel. It can be natural or it can be reprocessed after it has been used. Some restaurants give their used vegetable oil to those that burn Biodiesel in their vehicles. Once it has been cleaned they are able to use it without harming their vehicle.

Some types of food items are grown in higher supply than the demand just so that ethanol can be produced. It is usually mixed with about 15% regular gasoline in order to make the mix work. It seems that many in the business of growing such food items though don't always agree with this use of it. They feel the foods should be used to feed those in need.

Biofuel is most commonly found in the form of a solid though. For example burning wood falls into this category. You can use it to cook with and to heat your home instead of relying upon natural gas. The downside though is that this can emit dangerous elements into the environment.

There is ongoing testing where the variables are being controlled right now in the area of biofuel. It is believed this type of renewable energy could one day be a breakthrough in the area of supplying fuel for our vehicles. Look for great things to be coming up in this area in the future.

If we can figure out an affordable process for using biofuel we can create more than half of what is depleted annually from our natural resources. This is what facts continue to motivate researchers to move forward and funders to continue with grant money to allow it to happen.

The one issue that seems to be a concern is that in order to generate more biofuel to use, there is a great deal of land that has to be accessed. That could mean land normally used for growing food and other resources is no longer available. A close eye will need to be kept in that particular area.

As some of this concern has come to light, other forms of biofuel to be able to use are being introduced. Since these natural products are able to give off heat that can be transferred to fuel. Even trash can be used to create biofuel. This means less of it will be around to remain in landfills.

One of the most successful biofuel companies out there is in Cedar Rapids, Iowa. It is known as BFC Gas & Electric. They are able to recycle approximately 150 tons of materials each day at their facility. They process wood remains from projects and from sawmills in the area.

There is also paper that is used instead of being wasted when it was used for projects and scraps remain. Sometimes there are types of paper and cardboard that can't be successfully recycled so it is processed here.

Crops that have been ruined, diseased plants and trees, and the corn stalks that remain after harvest all work as well. More than 40,000 homes in the Cedar

Rapids area are provided with electricity from this particular company. They are really working hard to put the use of biofuel to work for the benefit for their community.

In some other areas the use of changing cow manure into biofuel is being done. This is something that not everyone finds appealing but it can be a viable way to get more benefits out of such waste. There are still many details of this type of biofuel to be worked out though.

Chapter 8

The Future of Renewable Energy

As you can see there will be plenty of benefits from all of these types of renewable energy. While they are all implemented right now on some level, there is still more that needs to be done. We need to learn how to get the maximum benefits from them.

At the same time we need to learn how to reduce the costs involved with getting that energy out of them. That seems to be the biggest hold up with getting them really rolling. The fact that they work and they reduce pollution is very positive aspects that encourage us to move forward with them.

As we come more aware of the fact that we are depleting our energy sources we need to take action now. The more we can learn not to depend on those resources the better off our entire world will be. Take your time to learn all you can about renewable energy too so you can be aware of what is going on around you.

Keep up on the developments that are taking place in these areas. It is actually quite fascinating and certainly something you will want to continue exploring. At the same time it is wise to take a close look at how you are using natural sources of energy.

Make cut backs where you can to continue conserving what we do have available right now to create the energy we often take for granted in our society. It doesn't mean you can't continue to enjoy your lifestyle, but rather try to view it from an environmentally friendly perspective.

There is some negativity out there though in regards to producing renewable energy. There is a concern about the amount of space it is going to take to get all of these methods into place. There is also the concern that some businesses will lose money as they won't be needed in full demand to harvest the fossil fuels. Yet the overall design of the turbines for windmills and for solar panels is an area where improvements can continue to be made.

If they don't have to take up as much room or be so noticeable more people will be willing to install them. Getting creative in this area is something we should encourage and that should be possible due to the technology we have readily available to us.

Some of the experts also worry that there will be some problems that arise but we aren't aware of them yet. However, that shouldn't prevent us from moving forward and getting all we can from these renewable energy sources. Crossing those bridges as they arise is the best course of action to take.

They are looking though along the lines of pollution and destruction due to the use of the types of construction equipment used to complete such projects. There is also a concern about the risk of the work too. Even with proper training people can get hurt or killed in the process of erecting them.

Some people aren't up for change and that includes how they get their energy. They are used to relying upon coal and natural gas. They are used to what they pay for these items and they are afraid to embrace something new. Continuing to provide them with accurate information though can really help them to understand the big picture that is here.

The possibilities that are open to us along the lines of renewable energy are huge. There is no limit to how far we can take them as long as they are going to benefit society as a whole. It will be very interesting to look back ten or twenty years from now and see how far the concepts of renewable energy have come.

Chapter 9

Conclusion

There seems to be more of an interest in the forms of renewable energy these days than ever before. People from all walks of life are seeing the many benefits it can offer. What should be an indicator that we need to continue moving forward is that many of the underdeveloped countries out there use more renewable energy than the rest of us.

While it is great that we have technology on our side, we need to always keep in mind what these products are doing to our environment. Global warming has always been a huge concern. The problem seems to continue to get worse though with the various types of pollution that are placed into the air.

This is believed to be a key factor in the strange things that go on around us with the weather. Desert areas have seen rain and snow in recent years. Areas that get substantial rainfall are now in a drought. Several natural disasters including hurricanes, floods, and tornadoes continue to destroy everything in their path.

As the governments out there as well as members of society continue to embrace what renewable energy has to offer it is likely that will start to come back into balance. There are plenty of major corporations out there leading the way as well. They want to set a very good example for others in the hopes that they will walk along the same path.

As the cost of fuel for our vehicles continues to increase everyone is worried about it. As a result it makes searching for an alternative form of renewable energy that can be used in place of it. Some of the vehicles out there known as hybrids do all this to help. They use solar power the majority of the time and only switch to gasoline as a backup until more solar energy can be collected.

By diversifying the various methods we use for renewable energy, we can balance out our desire to move forward as a society with the best of everything with our responsibility to protect the environment. There are many pros and cons to each of the renewable energy sources, but the benefits certainly outweigh the negativity.

There is no way around the fact that we can't replace the fossil fuel we consume. The more we do so the less that will be available for future generations. We can act on what we known and go with renewable energy or we can act selfish and continue to deplete what we have and leave the future generations to figure it out on their own.

www.ingramcontent.com/pod-product-compliance
Lightning Source LLC
LaVergne TN
LVHW010304200726
843506LV00014B/3386